CUPID'S
Bow

CUPID'S
Bow

ASHLEY E CLYKE

ARPress
ILLUMINATING IDEAS
EMPOWERING VOICES

ARPress
45 Dan Road Suite 36
Canton MA 02021

Hotline: 1(800) 220-7660
Fax: 1(855) 752-6001

Ordering Information:
Quantity sales. Special discounts are available on quantity purchases by corporations, associations, and others. For details, contact the publisher at the address above.

Printed in the United States of America.

ISBN-13:	Paperback	979-8-89389-806-4
	eBook	979-8-89389-807-1

Library of Congress Control Number: 2024923280

Contents

Pink Satin Sheets

In the chamber
in the shadows and candlelight
Pink Satin Sheets
move as flames
dance round
us indulging in -delight

Delight as known by us two
tumbling in the satin
doing things we shouldn't do

You laugh
as I kiss you
you Scream
when I sigh
You pursue
you don't have to
come to me-
aye. aye. aye.

Connect

We connect
like we're free
There's more to
love
This Love
than sexdreams
It's deep in my eyes
I see it in yours
-this power struggle
this echoing silent roar.
We're fighting-us
Closing doors.
shoving to get away,
playing 'cause we're torn.
Lost and looking, searching
-Dividing

Using this physical
Relationship
To buy time
'cause we're hiding.
I need you by now,
You've been here too long
I gave you my heart.
And babe I know I'm not wrong.

My Way

You know,
being with you makes me
think.
Why are we never alone?
-I think you're shy.
You are always being
the proper guy.

I'm not so genteel
I'm naughty when I'm real.

I can give you a thrill
push you past
release, until…
Well, never mind
not a lot of men
can handle my kind-
caught your eye
Is It Interest

That I spy?
-a smile like that
Can leave a girl
Mesmerized.
Well, time to go home
-Don't worry,
I won't roam.

What,
You want me to stay.
Oh, you nasty boy
I thought you would see things my way.

Afterlust

Slow pull on a cigarette.

smoke drifting

clouds forming

tension Pulsing

Us In Bed

the afterlust

clears

my

head.

He-he

I'm new here, will you show me
around? You foreign
exciting new friend
I've found.
I don't speak the language
But I understand you.
Interesting.
You're understanding me too.
I love
What I've seen
I had fun you did too
It's not over yet?
I should still follow you
Such a nice place to eat
This wine and that tune

Come back to your house?
You're being naughty
Aren't you.
I'm not sure

I should.
-But nothing fun
Happens to me.
So
You show the way
And I'll follow
He-he.

What Would You Do

I saw you down the hall
I know your number
I should call.
But what would you say
come over
and would I stay.

If I knock on your door,
would you invite me in,
should I give up to chance
that we might spend the night
in carnal sin.
Awkward seduction
The look in my eye
would you sense it,
would you answer my cry.
would you feel
the thick layer
of sweat on my skin

Would you taste the exotic spice-
That flavors my lips-
would you take your hands
down
over
and past
the curve of my hips

Bend me over
And would you make a move.

Rip off my clothes.

What would you do?

By The Water

By the water
Leaf and Grass
A silhouette
-your slender figure's
lines are cast

chaste

innocent

-Virginal,

my timid soul endeavors to ask

yet in your presence

a coward I am, and flown is the chance.

Please

Allow to me

High Natures Prize

Your Love

Your Beauty

and the courage I can't find.

Gentle Love

gentle lover

gentle, man

pleasing touch

caring hand

gently hard, gently firm

fixed and steady

strong and learned

true

seduction

soft

delay

temperate

love

don't go

Remain.

Sex

Sex
What you want
What you get

Sex
Reasons why
'Cause we met

Sex
Sex can be
Deliberate

Sex
Flavors life
-And it ain't over yet

Sex!

Black

lost in Black.
Black
silky fleece-
I've lost myself.

in torrents
completely-

In such that
I can not hide.

Exquisite the feeling

touching your body
kissing
reeling
never before

am I found?

it's deceiving

Persuasive you are

And To this fleece you did lead me

Black fleece

Through which you can see me.

Sow What You Reap

You said goodbye
For the tenth time.
But
You come back,
Then
You leave

I Use You Too.
Aswell.

We are entwined in a passionate
Spell.

Hard, Soft, Sweet,
-you treat me like a piece of
Meat.

And I have my revenge
Ignore me, you'll see-
I'm what you need
Remember dear Lover
You sow what you reap.

Would you? Why Not?

"You know what?
I just noticed,
You're my type
You are actually very
Hot."

"would you with me?"

Why

Why not?

Should we

Could we?

Can we

Would we?

I wouldn't mind.

Let's give it a try...

Okay.

I can't believe
this is how
We
Decide.

Honey

Golden honey
has us
For Used Instead of Oil.
-the sword and the sheath
would have spoiled.

Sticky golden syrup
Smack Smack
Pleasuring what's yours
And mine
-and in this honey
We are stuck in a love
Trap.

Yet, honey is not
used for this.
BUT for my sword
and for your sheath-
To explain what I mean

Honey
Is the
State
Of lust
That sword and sheath
Must have. They must.

Do You Care To Dance With Me

I hear a song
When we're together
It's sweet I'm listening
But so far we
Just sit together
And don't do
Anything.

I'm going to
Take a chance
And ask
Please answer honestly
On my bed I love to dance
Do you care to dance with me?

Ripe

I want you
Now
So
I'll get your attention
Ready for this
Here's a bold suggestion

I'm ripe.

Pick me.
I'm Good for your Digestion

Those

Those
Private
Sexy
Pleasures.
Kept in,
Secret
Black
Intimate-
places that renders.
When
Lace that comes
undone
-with

Lust

That does

Engulf and succumb

Reveals

That

What was pure

And enjoys

That what has

Become.

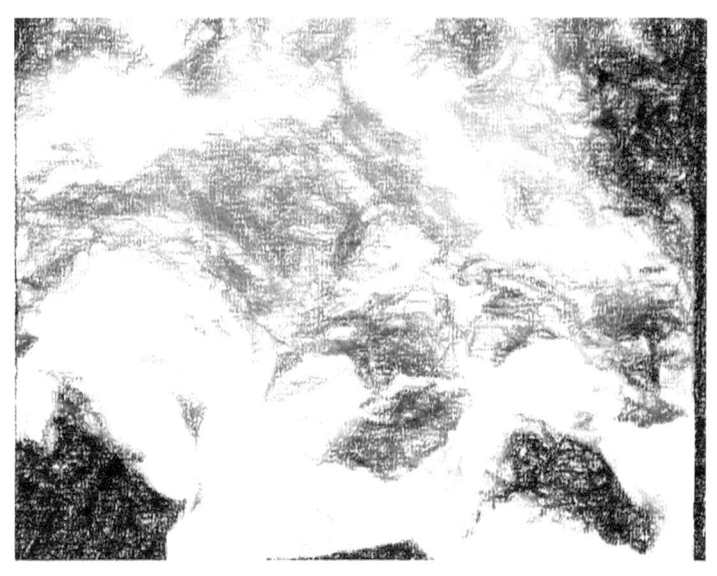

Rock Hard

You're
ROCK HARD
stiff and stern
just smack me
babe- teach
I'll learn.

Saddle up!
Rough and tough
BRONCO RIDE
Search my stuff.

Rugged, bold
Hot and cold
You are
A masterpiece
Who's In control.

Naturally

Follow me
Let's shake the trees
Get lost
in the
undergrowth.
I feel the need
To Be naked and free
Like Animals
Mating
Doing it
Naturally.

What Do You Mean

"What do you mean?

RACY raunchy, dirty, down low and WET. hands in butter. chicken BREAST. oil springs, a MATTRESS. Overwhelming MUSKY SCENT. sweat,a ride, -stopping- SPENT. a tug. a grip. CONDIMents. salt and pepper—add some spice, mixing paint, BLOW on dice, Jackpot Round!. HORN make sound. giddy up.
horse to MOUND.

"Get It?"

Human Body

the
Human body?
-we have them,
Right?
Excellent!
You are bright.
and what
are they
for?
Come now
You must know of
Some more.
Of What is
Their Purpose?
What potential
They have stored?
The service they
Provide ?
Well now,
Of course you must know

There are
Male and female
And low and behold
one
Is
Like a glove.
And the other
Has
A tail.

Put them together
And what do they
share ? – Love

Right.

Yes my beautiful
Who is as keen as a dove
Let me demonstrate
And we will make love!

Hey Girl

Mmm, I'm So
H O R N Y.

"Hey girl – look at that man!"
-that man so hot,
when he writes a check
the watermarks get
WET.

"Lay it on me Sugar!"
that's it, I see you looking
at me.
You want some of this?
It's E A S Y!
-"you just come over here, now".

I'll give it to you
-I'll give it to you –Good!

! I AIN'T LYING !
You know you want some of This
Everyone wants some of This
-I Want Some of This.

Look at you laughing
-come back!
Come Back Here

?how are we going to
get together if
you're leaving?

"Damn, Girl"

I'm sure that
was my soulmate
who just walked
by

-"Why you laughing?"

You shouldn't be laughing at me
I'm going to marry that man someday
-Laughing at me.

Like you could do any better.
,
You couldn't pick up a man
If you were the last free taxicab
At an Airport.

HA!
…
…
…
…
…

The Seaman Said

A stormy
night
In a drinking hole.

Near the Harbor
The truth unfolds…

The Seaman said,
With a glint in his eye,
"Listen Dearie, this is why."
because
I can kiss you.
tease you,
and
Leave you.

Friends with benefits.
I can even retrieve you.

This is my right

love's to much for reason.

I want a life that's
Colored like seasons.

-Where I do what I want.
-Say what I please.
-Arrive and depart.
Sail on the breeze.

There was a ship
With crew men Free.
-they visit every port,
Because they sail the seven seas.

As The Flower Petals Fly

As the flower petals fly.
Yield like a branch of the cherry blossom tree.
I
Am
The Wind.
That pollinates, bringing you
Your seed.

Yield until
The
Petals
Dance and fly because of me.

Molding Clay

Form

Take shape

Become and obey.

Give.

Make ready.

Be my molding clay.

Do It To Me

Do it to me
Do it to me

Do it to me Good.
Do it as I imagine
Set fire to the wood
Crude, sticky sap
Smoke in a smothering flame
Do it to me
Do it to me
Fire
Blaze! Blaze! Blaze!

You Pirate

Like
On a Ship
On the sea
I am captive
You captivate me
Approach me
Touch me
Be private.
My treasures
Are
Hidden
Undress me
Ravage me
Take me prisoner
You
Pirate.

Try

Now closer
Come hither.
You know I can see right through you.
-Thinking of how now to seduce me?
Why not? it is a good idea.
Test me, if you do it wouldn't hurt.
You're Thirsty .
I'm Quenching.
Try, I'm tempting

Here I am
Right before you
-read my mind, I've tequila at home
and a key to my
room

Don't be shy Sexy Lover
If you knew the things I'd do to you.

In The Place

In the place that hides my secrets,
you taste my treasures for
private reasons,
gently your touch leaves me in pleasure, have
my body
raw
Intense.
release,
release me,

That's better.

How You Do Trust Me

How you do trust me,
eat from my hand.
closer I approach
touch me, kiss.
Beautiful
We're man and woman.

Open

Hey, Sexy.
Open.
Let me inside
You've been swimming
'round
The fishbowl
Of
My mind.
I'll be fish feed.
You
Nibble a bit
And after your
Hooked.
I'll let you have
It.

Now

Now,
Here's my number.
I know you won't
Call.
But
When you want sex,
I'll
Look better
That's all.

Secret Meat

Oh, I can!
I'm delish
Sex with me
A gourmet dish.

I'll serve you
Up
Drink you
From a Styrofoam
Cup.
Fries and gravy
Dip, Repeat.
Get your hands dirty
When you
Eat

Smother you
With so much sauce
You'll fly like a
Side salad
That you
Toss.
Too much sweet
A tasty treat
Chocolate, Cheese
And
Secret meat.

Pants

Pants
You should be my pants
No,
You should be in my pants-
Like you're pants.
Like you're tight,
Close fitting
Pants.
The kind of pants
That
Rides up and makes you
Uncomfortable
Pants

The kind that
Gets in between
The places that are
Personal and pleasurable
Pants.
Maybe even
Coveralls.
But definitely
Pants.

Lucky

We'll get in trouble
You whisper back
When I say do it in the bathroom

You're so timid
And I like that
When I'm with you the world seems to relax

I spend time
Thinking
And you know what I find?

That I'm the luckiest person

With you I'm alive.

Own Me

Love
You sexy beast
You thought that
You owned me
But I'm still
Wild and free
Try
Try to attain
Try to possess
The minx that you see
You can acquire
But never own in confidence

Enchanting

Enchanting…
The part where
She kisses him
And they tumble
Onto the bed
His hand beneath
Her head
Her lips pressed
Against his
When he lifts up
Her dress
And enters
Aware of nothing
But her heaving
Bosom
And the fire
In her
That he must
Put to rest.

Only You

I love you so, and I am caught.
Caught!
-with no ability to manage escape
-because of you.
ONLY YOU
Everything is "all of you"

That charges this-
Pulsing rhythm
That races from out
my heart
In this hole
This well, this water bucket
I sit in
Submerged in Blissful Insanity